# INTRODUCTION

Nowadays we get many books and podcasts on starting a new business, which claim to cover every aspect of business planning. But Brannback and Carsrude take a unique approach. They guide new and experienced entrepreneurs through the startup and business process, speaking in the voice of an experienced and wise advisor. They emphasize what entrepreneurs should know and why. Their book provides an engaging and informative understanding of the startup process, without any tedium and complexity. This book is an invaluable resource for students who are interested in pursuing business as a career.

• **Mr. Sandip Patel, BBA Student,
Amity University Online, Noida, India**

"Brannback and Carsrude present a comprehensive and engaging approach to starting and growing a business, explaining in simple language the context, mindset, and behaviors required to become an entrepreneur. We have also included global examples of many successful businesses and their behaviors in this book,
So that the readers can understand them easily. Along with this, we have also prepared a list of recommended practices, which will make it even easier for you to read and understand."

"Ultimately, this book is for everyone who wants to build a real business or a real career that meets their goals, and not just make imaginary business plans. This book breaks the traditional myths in India about startups, and it helps everyone to become an entrepreneur and realize their dreams. Brännback and Carsrud have written a very important book, which is a must-read for students, entrepreneurs, or anyone who wishes to take advantage of opportunities and achieve their goals. This book will also be included in the curriculum."

"Reading this book proved to be like a booster dose for my BBA course. This book not only reminded me of many of my mistakes, but also taught me that if you want to start your own business, read this first. It is a tool that will help you save both time and money. Before publishing, we gave this book to professors, students, entrepreneurs and authors, who found it to be an important tool that can prove to be extremely useful for any startup or new entrepreneur."

# CONTENTS

Introduction
Introduction   1
Myths and Stories of Entrepreneurship   3
Entrepreneurship and Importance of Dreams   5
There is no one story   7
The Story of Peter Thorvaste   9
Josiah Wedgwood and his success story   10
A legacy of entrepreneurship   11
importance of dreams and complexity of technological inventions   13
Historical development and modern significance of entrepreneurship   15
wider implications of entrepreneurship and debunking myths   17
Widespread influence and regional development of Birch's studies   20
National innovation systems and the impact of entrepreneurship   22
broader perspective on the role of new venture incubators and accelerators   25
Prevalence of entrepreneurship and definition of success   27
Who is an entrepreneur?   29

| | |
|---|---|
| Entrepreneurship and the influence of personality | 31 |
| The Mindset and Attitudes of Entrepreneurs | 33 |
| Defining Entrepreneurship? | 36 |
| Opportunity Recognition | 38 |
| Entrepreneurial Goals | 41 |
| different goals for different people | 43 |
| Other definitional issues | 45 |
| self employed entrepreneurs | 47 |
| Reference for self-employed entrepreneurs | 49 |
| A False Dualism | 52 |
| Do the goals differ? | 55 |
| A Mini-Case Example | 57 |
| Opportunities & Entrepreneurship | 59 |
| Practice | 61 |
| What is it to be successful? | 62 |
| Why check for success? | 64 |
| Defining success | 67 |
| Defining Failure | 71 |
| Measurement issues in defining success/failure | 74 |
| Success in an entrepreneurial context | 77 |
| In-depth analysis of firm founding success | 79 |
| Comprehensive approach | 82 |
| ancient story of success | 84 |
| Success and opportunities | 86 |
| Linking success to entrepreneurial goals | 89 |
| Is success the same as wealth? | 92 |
| Networking Rules for Networking | 94 |
| | 97 |

Success means enjoying
An inspiring example from Italy 99

# Why?

From the beginning, I have been passionate about entrepreneurship. Since childhood, I always had entrepreneurship ideas in my mind. When I started my first venture, I was very excited, but it failed. I tried again, then failed again. But every time I fell, I learned to stand up again. Amidst these ups and downs, I realized that I needed to prepare myself better. So I started part-time training in big companies of India like Reliance, Airtel, and State Bank of India. Along with this, I also worked with startups.

In 2023, I realized that just like I made mistakes, there would be

many others who would be wasting both time and money due to lack of the right advice. I felt that the books and podcasts available in the market are not updated with the changing technology. So I decided that I would share my struggle and learnings through a book to those who aspire to become entrepreneurs or who are already in entrepreneurship.

This journey has been extremely challenging for me, but I accepted this challenge, and the result is this book. Many authors and professors who write books on entrepreneurship teach entrepreneurship, but I have actually started a business. Because of this I have a different perspective. In this book I have tried to present my thinking with reality and practicality.

Many of my students have also contributed to writing this book, who have established different types of businesses. This book is not only based on the theory of entrepreneurship, but is also full of real life experiences and examples. I have expressed my deep respect and love for the world of entrepreneurship through this book.

I hope that this book will instill a new hope in the readers and inspire them to adopt entrepreneurship as a career. The joy of starting a business, the satisfaction of the first sale, and the experience of facing challenges – you will find all this in this book.

Through this book, I will introduce you to the steps and tips necessary to become a successful entrepreneur. In the world of business it is important to challenge the rules and sometimes even break them. As Anglican bishop Alan Wilson said-

> "If Nobody Ever Tries To Go Beyond The Rules, The Rules Will Never Change. And That Is The Process Of Evolution."

This Book Has Been A Personal And Professional Journey For Me, In Which The Business Owners And Seniors Who Have Worked With Me Have Also Contributed A Lot. It Has Been An Amazing Experience To See The Evolution Of Business And Technology Over The Last Several Years, And I Am Grateful To All Those Who Guided Me Along The Way.

Finally, I Would Also Like To Thank My Family, Who Supported My Efforts And Motivated Me To Face Reality. Every Successful Entrepreneur Must Know How To Maintain A Work-Life Balance, And This Balance Is An Important Part Of This Journey.

After Reading This Book, I Hope You Too Will Be Able To Muster The Courage To Step Into The World Of Business, And Move Towards Becoming A Successful Entrepreneur.

# What?

Through this book, we will try to explain in detail to you "What is Business?" in the first chapter and its various roles in the global economy. Our aim is not only to provide a general introduction to business activities, but also to look at the historical and philosophical foundations that make this book unique and deeply informative.

To understand the relationship between business and the economy, it is essential that we understand the historical context of the subject. History teaches us how trade and business have shaped societies, and the philosophical perspective leads us to consider what the purpose of business is and in what direction it should develop.

We adopt this approach because we believe it is extremely important to challenge your preconceived notions based on solid facts and principles. This book will inspire you to reconsider the foundations that you have previously believed to be true.

Through this book, we will present you with an analytical view of various aspects of business, including the importance of entrepreneurship, ethics, social responsibility, and its role in the global market. We will also give you some examples that will explain how becoming a businessman or starting a successful business is not only about economic gain but also has a larger purpose of bringing a positive change in society.

This way, this book will not only provide information about business and entrepreneurship but will also help you to become thoughtful and broaden your perspective. We will try to make this book a guide for you that will not only enrich your knowledge but also lead you to success in your business life.

# INTRODUCTION

Entrepreneurship is not just limited to starting a business; it is the art of innovation, risk-taking and creating something new. It involves identifying opportunities in the market, mobilising resources and taking risks wisely to build a successful venture. Entrepreneurs are the prime movers of economic growth, who constantly challenge conventions and find creative solutions to problems.

In simple terms, entrepreneurship is the art of turning ideas into reality. It is about having the vision to see possibilities where others see only obstacles, and about showing determination to pursue those possibilities, no matter what the challenges are. Whether it is a small startup or a large enterprise, entrepreneurship requires a combination of creativity, patience and strategic thinking.
Nowadays, wherever you go in any corner of the world, be it a newspaper, magazine like Financial Times, The Hindu, Money Control, or Zee Enterprise, or any business channel you watch on TV, one thing is certain—political leaders or economists will be seen presenting their views on the importance of business and industry development. At the national level, the topic is constantly discussed about how business and business development is important for a country's economy.

Amidst these discussions and reports, you will often find additional information about business or an inspirational story of a businessman. However, many of us often ignore the information of these leaders or economists, and our attention is focused on the fascinating stories that tell about the hard struggle of a brave businessman or a successful entrepreneur.

We sometimes enjoy speeches or stories that highlight failures—whether on TV or in the form of award-winning movies like The Social Network. For example, the stories of the founders of Facebook in 2010 and Apple in 2013 were very popular. As Kaufman, of Kansas City, Missouri, recently said:

> *Entrepreneurship is the heartbeat of any nation's economy. It not only creates jobs but also drives innovation and competition, positively impacting society as a whole.*

Thus, entrepreneurship is not just a story of individual success; it is a comprehensive process of development of society and economy. It contains lessons learnt through failures and challenges. It is this process that has made many of today's great entrepreneurs reach their heights.

In this chapter, we will not only understand the basics of entrepreneurship but also look at examples that have proved how taking risks and showing courage can yield sweet results. Through these stories, you will also learn how determination and efforts in the right direction are required to turn an idea into reality.

# MYTHS AND STORIES OF ENTREPRENEURSHIP

Entrepreneurship stories often fall into two categories. One is about a person who had a unique idea that few people understood or believed in. But that person, through sheer determination and perhaps luck, found himself in the right place at the right time. And then what happened? It became a spectacular success story! There is also some drama in the story to make it more interesting.

Often the story is about a successful entrepreneur who rose from poverty to riches through hard work and the ability to make the right decisions at the right time. But, "dropping out of college to become an entrepreneur" hasn't always been the only myth of entrepreneurship. In this book, we'll explore some other entrepreneurial models.

For example, Hollywood has adapted the stories of great entrepreneurs such as Henry Ford and Thomas Alva Edison into movies. But Hollywood has yet to bring to the screen the stories of famous women entrepreneurs such as Madam C.J. Walker. Madam C.J. Walker turned her homemade hair and scalp care recipes into a business empire and became the first self-made black female millionaire in the United States in the early 1900s.

The second type of story is about a local or national entrepreneur who is celebrating fifty years in business and is now passing the firm on to the next generation. These stories are popular because they are spectacular and entertaining. Many of us are personally familiar with their products or services, and you may even know these entrepreneurs personally.

These stories are interesting because they show us how "dreams come true." Have any of these entrepreneurs inspired you personally? Ask yourself if reading any of these stories or watching the films made you dream that you too could become an entrepreneur?

You don't have to be a dropout from a top college to become an entrepreneur. Nor do you need to be under 60 or already rich, as we will show in this book.

# ENTREPRENEURSHIP AND IMPORTANCE OF DREAMS

Sigmund Freud believed that dreams and words can have many meanings. Like the word "dream," this word also comes with both good and bad meanings. The word "dream" is believed to have originated from the German word "draigmus," which means deception, illusion, or apparition. It may also be related to the Norse word draiger (ghost, spirit) or even the Sanskrit word "druh," which means an attempt to harm or hurt someone.

Have you ever thought that your entrepreneurial dream could also become one of these stories? Elias Howe (1819-1867) said that he was inspired to invent the sewing machine from a dream in which cannibals were attacking him with spears. The spears matched the design of the sewing machine needles he had designed for his machine.

Nikola Tesla is also said to have been able to visualize a device in his lifetime. He could see and create a plan in his "mind's eye" without writing it down. It was a kind of "daydreaming".

Biographies of self-made billionaires often become bestsellers because they tell stories of dreams coming true. For example, the biography of Steve Jobs and the dramatic events that took place at the beginning of Apple, or the film based on the life of Mark Zuckerberg, which tells the story of the birth of Facebook.

While many of these stories tend to focus on men, women's entrepreneurship stories cannot be overlooked either. For example, Coco Chanel (fashion), Madame C.J. Walker, Elizabeth Arden, Dame Anita Roddick and Estée Lader (cosmetics), Olive En Beach (airplanes), Oprah Winfrey and Martha Stewart (media), or Ruth Handler (who gave us "Barbie" and co-founded Mattel Toys).

There are many famous entrepreneurs in the world whose names we may not be familiar with, but who have been extremely successful in their fields. For example, Ingvar Kamprad of Sweden (Ikea), Gerard Adrien Heineken of the Netherlands (Heineken beer), or Don Melchor de Santiago Concha y Toro and his wife Emiliana Subercaseaux of Chile (winery), or Takeshi Mitarai of Japan (Canon Electronics).

All of these entrepreneurs have a common trait. They are visionary, hardworking, risk takers, ambitious, with exceptional leadership skills. Their never-say-die attitude makes them a source of inspiration. These qualities, combined with a brilliant idea and marketing ability, build a great company, which eventually makes entrepreneurs very rich.

But is money the only definition of success? For many of these entrepreneurs, success meant transforming an industry, or doing something that was sustainable and lasting for generations.

For those who know about successful entrepreneurship, these companies are a source of inspiration. It is not just limited to new technology or internet businesses (like Apple, Dell, Amazon or eBay). Entrepreneurship is also about sustainability over time.

# THERE IS NO ONE STORY

Take the example of the great engineer and scientist Nikola Tesla. He donated the patents for many of his inventions and often preferred to be alone. Tesla had a unique definition of success. For him, success did not just mean making money. One way to make money might be to create value for customers by selling an idea, but that cannot be the only definition of success.

There are many ways to measure success. It depends on the perspective from which you look at life and the goals you set for yourself. This is the perspective we consider successful entrepreneurship. This is often how a successful entrepreneur is described. The meaning of success is in the eye of the beholder and depends on the goals the entrepreneur sets for himself.

We will discuss the entrepreneurial mindset and this definition of success in more depth later in this book.

If you had to name some successful entrepreneurs today, you would probably name Steve Jobs, Michael Dell, Martha Stewart, Mark Zuckerberg, Oprah Winfrey, and Henry Ford. This is because you know their products, use them, and are familiar with the success of their businesses.

But you may not be familiar with the names Peter Thorvaste, Josiah Wedgwood, Erling Persson, Billy Durant, or Anita Radic. However, many of you know, use, or own products from the companies these founders founded: scissors from Fiskars, china dishes from Wedgwood, clothing from H&M, cars from General Motors, or cosmetics from The Body Shop.

# THE STORY OF PETER THORVASTE

Consider Petter Thorvaste, who founded Fiskars Ironworks in 1649. Today the company is known as Fiskars and produces not only orange-handled scissors but also garden tools, ceramics, and boats.

Fiskars today is a leading global supplier of branded consumer products for the home, garden, and outdoor spaces. The Fiskars brand palette also includes brands such as Iittala, Royal Copenhagen, Rørstred, Arabia, Buster, and Gerber.

All of these entrepreneurs are proof that success is not just about money. These are people who transformed industries and built businesses that have endured for generations.

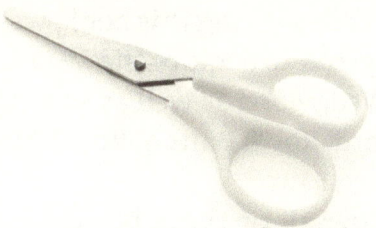

# JOSIAH WEDGWOOD AND HIS SUCCESS STORY

Josiah Wedgwood was an English potter who founded the Wedgwood Pottery firm in 1759. His firm's products are still sold today, and the "Wedgwood China" brand (which includes the Waterford Crystal line) is known around the world for its quality (see Figure 1.2). This is a great example of how an entrepreneur's vision and hard work can lead to a brand that lasts for generations.

While writing this book, we learned that on May 11, 2015, Fiskars agreed to acquire the WWRD Group. The WWRD Group includes Wedgwood as well as several other luxury brands, such as Waterford, Royal Dalton, Royal Albert, and Rogaaska.

Now all of these brands have become part of the same family firm, Fiskars, in Finland. This is a great reminder that successful entrepreneurs can create enterprises and products that continue to influence the business world and the lives of consumers several hundred years later.

# A LEGACY OF ENTREPRENEURSHIP

This story teaches us that entrepreneurship is not limited to the success of one person, but it is a legacy that lasts for many generations. As the examples of Wedgwood and Fiskars show, when an entrepreneur has a strong vision and is committed to his work, his impact is not limited to his lifetime.

This definition of success lies in the quality, reliability, and long-term sustainability that comes with a brand and its products.

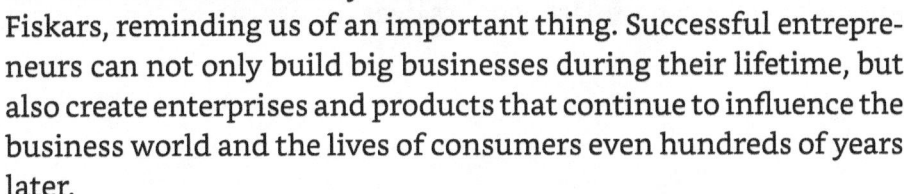

All of these brands are now part of the Finnish family firm Fiskars, reminding us of an important thing. Successful entrepreneurs can not only build big businesses during their lifetime, but also create enterprises and products that continue to influence the business world and the lives of consumers even hundreds of years later.

For example, the Heinz brand is best known today for its ketchup. But, very few people know that Heinz's first successful product was not ketchup, but pickled horseradish. Heinz's famous logo '57 Varieties' was created in 1896, which remains an identity among people even today. Not only this, this logo was also the first electric sign lit on Manhattan in 1900, symbolizing the latest technology of the time.

However, in recent times HJ Heinz has been bought by Warren Buffett's Berkshire Hathaway and 3G Capital from the founding family. This also tells us how brands and companies founded by big entrepreneurs become part of other big companies over time, yet their influence and identity remains.

Then there is the story of Henry Ford and his Ford Motor Company. Henry Ford not only revolutionised manufacturing processes but also completely transformed the automotive industry. His thinking and his company's strategies were so influential that they set a new benchmark for mass production and modern industrial practices.

Ford Motor Company remains largely under family control today through a complex ownership structure. This means that the control and influence of a big brand like Ford remains in the hands of the family that started it generation after generation.

All these examples make it clear that when entrepreneurship has sustainability, it becomes a legacy not just for the present but also for the future. These brands were not just built for profits but show that products and enterprises built with the right approach and hard work can impact people's lives for centuries.

# IMPORTANCE OF DREAMS AND COMPLEXITY OF TECHNOLOGICAL INVENTIONS

We all dream, and many times our dreams become the foundation of future inventions. For some people, these dreams become the inspiration for invention and innovation, leading to new ideas that change the world. When we talk about technological inventions, Thomas A. Edison is the first name that comes to mind. Edison was not only a great inventor but also an amazing entrepreneur who dreamed of bringing electric light to homes and made it come true. He founded power generation companies that still bear his name. Even a giant company like General Electric (GE) was founded by Edison.

However, the story of electricity is incomplete without Tesla. Nikola Tesla, often known for the development of alternating current (AC), was a pioneer in the field of technological innovation. While Edison's team was focusing on direct current (DC), Tesla worked on new technology like alternating current, which revolutionized the field of electricity.

It is worth noting that not all successful inventions are the result of the efforts of a single person, but many people have contributed to them. For example, 22 other people tried to invent the light bulb before Edison. But Edison understood the power of marketing and branding and successfully brought it to the market. This means that to make an invention successful, not only technical knowledge but also business acumen is required.
Often the pioneers in an industry like Tesla are not the ones who win the awards, money, or accolades. Rather, it is the ones who come later and figure out how to commercially leverage that invention. Being successful is not always about taking the first step. As some say, sometimes the one who tries first gets left behind by the other pioneers.

For any entrepreneur, a vital part of success is inspiring his team around a shared dream. Entrepreneurship starts with just one person's idea, but to make it successful, it is important to expand that idea within the entire team and commercialize it.

# HISTORICAL DEVELOPMENT AND MODERN SIGNIFICANCE OF ENTREPRENEURSHIP

We are going to get a little academic here, so forgive us. It is important to understand that the terms 'entrepreneurship' and 'entrepreneur' have existed for centuries. Some believe that the term was first mentioned by Cantillon in his work in 1755. Some consider Say (1803) to be the earliest figure in the theory of entrepreneurship. Hoselitz (1951) found the roots of the term in historical contexts of the Middle Ages. One of the oldest and most common meanings is "celui qui entrepend quelquez choses," which literally means "one who acts." In simple terms, the term refers to an active person.

In history, the term entrepreneurship has given rise to many academic debates. However, Joseph Schumpeter (1934) is considered as the intellectual father of modern entrepreneurship. He believed that an entrepreneur is someone who pursues innovation and turns it into a business.

The importance of entrepreneurship in contemporary life grew especially in 1987. In this year, entrepreneurship was considered a key factor in national wealth creation, far more than just individual wealth creation. In 1987 David Birch published his book "Job Creation in America". The book was the result of a study conducted at MIT (Massachusetts Institute of Technology) between 1969 and 1986. Birch's study revealed that small start-up companies created more than 80% of new jobs in the United States, while large companies caused job losses.

This study shows that small companies have a greater chance of expansion than large companies. If large companies have to create jobs, it is usually through the formation of a new business unit, not through a completely new firm. For example, the owner of a small shop opened a second store under the supervision of his daughter, thereby creating new jobs.

Data from the United States Small Business Administration also confirms the fact that 99.5% of all companies in most Western countries are classified as small companies. This fact applies not only to the United States, but also to countries such as Australia, Chile, India and Finland.

In 2015, the United States saw an average of 310 new entrepreneurs added each month per 100,000 adults. This figure was up from a monthly average of 280 in 2014, indicating that entrepreneurship levels have returned to normal patterns after the Great Recession of 2008.

It is also interesting that in 2013, according to the US Census Bureau, 23 million people were self-employed. For whatever reason, more and more people are choosing different paths to becoming entrepreneurs.

# WIDER IMPLICATIONS OF ENTREPRENEURSHIP AND DEBUNKING MYTHS

The results of the study conducted by Burch challenged the long-held belief that large organizations are the engines and drivers of the national economy in terms of job creation, innovation, and growth. A follow-up study after Burch's study was presented by Bruce Kirchhaupt and Bruce Phillips. This study confirmed Burch's findings. During recessions, small companies played a significant role in creating new jobs, while large organizations often laid off people.

This finding was shocking to the general public and politicians. These results caught the attention of politicians and legislators. As reported by Brannback et al. (2014), every US president since Ronald Reagan has supported entrepreneurship and growth in his speeches. In 2001, the European Union (EU) signed the Lisbon Treaty, recognizing entrepreneurship as an important means of economic development and promising to give it extensive support.

In recent years, the term entrepreneurship has become so widely used that it has become difficult to say who is not an entrepreneur. In this chapter, we will discuss the definition of entrepreneurs and their characteristics.

In this book, we want to challenge the myths that view entrepreneurship from a limited perspective. The first myth is that entrepreneurship is only for a certain group of people, or that it is a career only for men. The second myth is that most entrepreneurs are already wealthy and are connected to the technology sector.

However, statistics show that this view is changing. The number of women entering entrepreneurship is growing faster than men. Moreover, entrepreneurship has also increased among the poor and the disabled in recent years. A prime example of this is the Grameen Bank, founded by Nobel Peace Prize winner Dr. Muhammad Yunus, which focused specifically on women.

Yunus believed that women were more capable of repaying loans than men and were less likely to waste money on risky ventures. His idea has played a key role in the economic empowerment of women around the world. The Women's World Bank is also pursuing the same concept.

Technology entrepreneurship has been popular for decades, and now more and more women are starting technology firms. There are many programs that encourage entrepreneurship. For example, companies like Google have been inspired by Stanford's Technology Ventures program.

Various universities in the United States also have special programs to encourage entrepreneurship. There are programs for military veterans at Syracuse University and UCLA, for social and green entrepreneurs at Colorado State University, and for people with disabilities at the University of Illinois at Chicago.

It is important to say that entrepreneurship is for everyone, regardless of their gender, race, sexual orientation, location, personal wealth, or physical condition. In this chapter, we want to inspire you to think about people who have chosen the path of entrepreneurship and made a difference despite living in different circumstances. Entrepreneurship can flourish in a variety of environments, and this shows that it can be a real option for everyone.

# WIDESPREAD INFLUENCE AND REGIONAL DEVELOPMENT OF BIRCH'S STUDIES

B irch's study also revealed that new firms that replace older firms tend to relocate and use different workforces and other resources, such as capital, transportation, government services, education, recreation, and energy. The study also predicted where the next "business hot beds" might emerge. One such example is Austin, Texas, which is known for its interesting mix of technology and artisanal entrepreneurship.

Birch proved that small firms and entrepreneurs are important to regional economic development, and subsequent studies have confirmed this conclusion. Some of the most famous examples include Silicon Valley and Route 128, which have become a model for other places around the world.

We are also seeing a resurgence of entrepreneurship in rust

belt cities like Detroit, which have had to reinvent themselves. For more on the importance of regional development, Saxenian's (1994) book Regional Advantage: Culture and Competition in Silicon Valley and Route 128 can be read.

Regional clusters of business activities and communities exist everywhere and are specific to certain industries or ecosystems. For example, today these even have their own annual trade shows, such as SXSW (South by Southwest), which attracts all the major actors in the Internet, interactive digital technology, music, and movies industries.

Another major example is the Consumer Electronics Show (CES), held annually in Las Vegas, where cutting-edge technology is usually launched. Similarly, the Detroit Auto Show is still dominated by the automobile industry, while the Paris Air Show is a major showcase for the aircraft industry.

These trade shows and exhibitions are considered important for regional development and global innovation. They not only spread new ideas but also showcase how different sectors and industries develop themselves and maintain their presence on a global scale.

# NATIONAL INNOVATION SYSTEMS AND THE IMPACT OF ENTREPRENEURSHIP

The development of national innovation systems was a result of Birch's findings. These systems are based on government initiatives to support the objectives of institutions. It is claimed that national innovation systems are created for the benefit of individual entrepreneurs, but research results are not conclusive on this. In many cases, these systems have proven to be merely theoretical and far-fetched for ordinary entrepreneurs.

It is important that we as individuals realize that entrepreneurship is not only related to job creation. It is also an important source of developing effective and innovative solutions to environmental and social problems. In many countries, cultural institutions, such as libraries, concert halls, universities, and foundations are named after successful entrepreneurs who have made significant donations to these organizations.

It is also necessary to understand that entrepreneurship is not limited to small firms. In fact, large organizations can also be highly entrepreneurial. This is often called "corporate entrepreneurship." In such cases, the entrepreneur himself does not come to the fore, but is identified as the innovator. In this context, entrepreneurship and innovation – or entrepreneur and innovator – become synonymous.

However, following Kirzner (1973), and in contrast to the views of Schumpeter (1934), innovation is not always essential to entrepreneurship as most people think. Since Birch's study, the issue of entrepreneurship and firm growth has been a topic of frequent discussion in government policies, academic research and the public media.

Although many people believe that entrepreneurship and development are synonymous terms, they are not always the same. Entrepreneurship and development do not always lead to good or successful results. As we have shown in this discussion, entrepreneurship can play a key role in the economic improvement of an individual, family, firm, region or nation. This means that entrepreneurship can exist not only in small firms but also in large organizations. It is also found in profit-making firms and non-profit social enterprises.

Although growth and innovation are often associated with entrepreneurship and entrepreneurial firms, this need not always be the case. Personal wealth creation does not always motivate an entrepreneur. In some cases, the motivation of entrepreneurs may be the desire to work independently, while in others it may be altruistic ambitions such as solving social problems.

Thus, the impact of entrepreneurship is not limited to the individual or business level. It can be a key element for social and economic development more broadly. The motivations and actions taken by entrepreneurs can have profound effects on society, sparking innovation, social change, and economic growth.

# BROADER PERSPECTIVE ON THE ROLE OF NEW VENTURE INCUBATORS AND ACCELERATORS

New venture incubators and accelerators play a vital role in the field of entrepreneurship. The purpose of these programs is to provide new entrepreneurs with support and resources to help them successfully establish their ventures. We have seen incubators and accelerators operate in a wide variety of industries, such as wireless technology, cell phone apps, biotechnology, agriculture, and the development of new food products.

Incubators and accelerators exist in the form of hundreds, if not thousands, of institutions and organizations around the world. Nearly every major research university has some sort of incubator or accelerator program running in or around it. For example, a high concentration of these activities can be seen in Silicon Valley and the Route 128 area of Boston, where efforts are made to attract and retain technical talent.

The main advantage of these programs is that they provide financial and business support to entrepreneurs at an early stage. For example, American television shows such as "Shark Tank" and its spin-off versions in other countries provide a platform for entrepreneurs to meet investors. This platform not only provides financial assistance but also offers business guidance and networking opportunities, thereby increasing the chances of success for new entrepreneurs.

However, it is hard to say whether incubators and accelerators actually help new ventures succeed. The evidence to date is divided on this. Many incubators and accelerators boast successful firms among their graduates, but it is also true that many successful firms are successful without the help of an incubator or accelerator. Therefore, participating in these programs is not a guarantee of success.

The truth is that the main basis for success in entrepreneurship is the entrepreneur's own hard work, dedication and determination. Just getting accepted into an incubator may be the first step towards success, but it is not the last step. It requires hard work, the right decisions and constant efforts.

There are also some scams in the incubator and accelerators industry. Therefore, entrepreneurs should make sure that the programs they are joining are reliable and transparent. Entrepreneurs should be cautious and use their network and experience to get the right information and guidance.

Finally, new venture incubators and accelerators can be a valuable resource for entrepreneurs, but relying solely on these programs is not enough for success. Entrepreneurs must put in their hard work, the right approach, and vigilance. With the right decisions and taking advantage of opportunities, they can steer their business to success.

# PREVALENCE OF ENTREPRENEURSHIP AND DEFINITION OF SUCCESS

As humans, we love stories, especially stories that show us that it is possible to be a financially successful entrepreneur. These stories inspire us, as most of these stories are well-known. We try to understand who an entrepreneur is and sometimes who the entrepreneurial collective or entrepreneurial team is through these stories. We believe that if we can define who an entrepreneur is, we can identify and encourage these people.

We often forget, or do not even consider, that the skills used in entrepreneurship are essential for success in any profession. Entrepreneurship is not limited to the field of business. A doctor, scientist, teacher, or social worker can also use entrepreneurial qualities and set their journey to success.

Success cannot be defined only by money. For many people, success means more than personal gain. For example, for Jonas Salk, who dedicated his life to eradicating polio, success meant developing a safe and effective vaccine, not achieving economic gain.

When asked who held the patent for his vaccine, he replied, "There is no patent. Can you patent the sun?" This statement reflects his mindset that his goals were not monetary. His aspirations included founding the Salk Institute in La Jolla, California, which continues to advance his vaccine work today.

Some consider Jonas Salk to be the symbol of early social entrepreneurship, even though the term "social entrepreneur" did not exist in his time. He worked for social welfare and focused on benefiting society rather than profits. Salk's example shows that entrepreneurship is not limited to business. It can also be a process of bringing positive change to society and achieving more important goals.

Entrepreneurship does not mean only earning money. It is a dedication to values and goals that are beneficial to society. Whether it is a tech startup, a scientific research, or a social initiative – the essence of entrepreneurship lies in people who want to make the world a better place through their efforts. We should adopt this broader perspective and look at entrepreneurship in its entirety.

# WHO IS AN ENTREPRENEUR?

In this discussion we try to understand who an entrepreneur is. According to the Global Entrepreneurship Monitor (GEM), entrepreneurs can be divided into two main categories: necessity entrepreneurs and opportunistic entrepreneurs. Necessity entrepreneurs are those who start a business because of their economic situation, such as to escape unemployment or hunger. On the other hand, opportunistic entrepreneurs are those who start a business by taking advantage of a market, invention, or opportunity.

In recent years, the United States has seen a rise in the number of entrepreneurs, especially those who are starting a business in response to an opportunity. This trend shows that today's new entrepreneurs are starting businesses not just to escape unemployment, but to take advantage of opportunities. This trend is particularly evident in immigrant communities, where the rate of new venture creation is higher than that of non-immigrants. Nearly 80% of new entrepreneurs are now opportunists, which is a significant increase compared to the years following the Great Recession.

In the late 1980s, academics began to focus on the definition of entrepreneurship. William Gartner challenged the concept of entrepreneurship in his 1988 article "Who is an Entrepreneur? Is This the Wrong Question?". He argued that it is not enough to define entrepreneurship based on personality alone. Instead, it is necessary to look at what entrepreneurs do, why they do it, and how they do it. Based on this understanding, academics assumed that if we could answer these questions, we should be able to design targeted educational programs that would help entrepreneurs succeed.

Many people believe that entrepreneurship is an innate quality that cannot be taught. Some explain this idea with the example of family businesses. But the reality is that succession in family businesses is one of the most difficult tasks. Not all children are willing or able to take over the business that their parents have established. At times, it happens that no successor is ready. Even after seeing the hard work of entrepreneurial parents, not all children wish to adopt that lifestyle.

The challenge of succession in family businesses shows that entrepreneurship does not come from family heritage alone. It is a combination of mindset, skills, and circumstances that make a person an entrepreneur. While some people may inherit entrepreneurship, others may develop it through their personal experiences and inspirations.

Entrepreneurship does not only mean starting a business, but it is a mindset that can help achieve success in any profession. Whether a person is an opportunistic entrepreneur or an entrepreneur born of necessity, the key to success lies in perseverance, innovation, and utilizing the right opportunities.

# ENTREPRENEURSHIP AND THE INFLUENCE OF PERSONALITY

The importance of personality for success in entrepreneurship is a hot topic. Some argue that being a successful entrepreneur is directly related to one's innate qualities. Certainly, it is important to have a personality compatible with the entrepreneurial life, but it does not depend only on personality. Rather, it is also influenced by many other factors, such as the idea, the market, and the culture in which the person is working.

It is often assumed that entrepreneurs are risk takers and innovators, but in reality this is not true in all cases. For example, certain personality types and motivational styles have been associated with entrepreneurship in Europe, the United States, and countries of the former British Empire. But this equation does not apply everywhere.

Attitudes towards entrepreneurship may vary in different cultures. The example of Persian Jews can illustrate that they chose the path of entrepreneurship because of their limited options. It was the only option available to them at the time. But these personality factors may not be equally effective in other cultures such as Asia, Latin America, or Africa.

Gender differences also influence entrepreneurship across cultures. So it is hard to say what makes a unique entrepreneurial personality. What we have learned is that the same qualities that make someone a successful entrepreneur can also make someone a successful pilot, scientist, or teacher.

Years of psychology research have shown that the traits of a successful entrepreneur in the United States and many countries in Europe are the same as those found in any other ambitious person, whether a lawyer, doctor, or airline pilot. To be successful, certain components of achievement motivation are necessary.

When it comes to entrepreneurs, this pattern may vary across cultures. But one component that seems to be common everywhere is the willingness to work hard. Another component is the willingness to learn new and different things. The role of the competitive personality may also change according to the cultural context, as these factors interact with each other.

This means that if you have the qualities needed to be a good scientist, lawyer, teacher, pilot, or other professional, you can use those qualities to succeed in entrepreneurship as well. Entrepreneurship is not just about risk-taking or innovation, but it also depends on hard work, a willingness to learn, and a mindset to excel in your field.

# THE MINDSET AND ATTITUDES OF ENTREPRENEURS

Success in the world of entrepreneurship is not limited to skill or opportunity. There is also a great difference in the mindset and attitude of entrepreneurs. Research by Branbank and Korsrud (2009) makes it clear that the entrepreneurial leadership style of successful entrepreneurs differs from that of ordinary entrepreneurs. The difference in these styles is also seen in the cognitive style, which determines how an entrepreneur views a problem and solves it.

In many cases, some of the skills associated with entrepreneurship can be taught. Therefore, entrepreneurial education is important, but it is not everything. There are certain qualities and attitudes that can be influenced by education, but some of these characteristics are close to art—a unique way of doing things that make a person unique. For a deeper understanding of the various aspects of entrepreneurial mindset, the topic has been discussed in detail in the edited volume by Korsrud and Branbank (2009).

Based on research, there is a strong belief that any individual who has the desire to discover opportunity and achieve his or her goal can become an entrepreneur. It is important to understand how much motivation and effort is required to achieve success. Success is not just about making money, but it also depends on one's personal approach. The definition of success may vary from person to person—for some it is about bringing about a positive change in society, while for others it is about achieving their dreams.

Entrepreneurship is an approach to life. It is not just the ability to create or lead a firm, but a way of understanding how entrepreneurs think. Entrepreneurs often view their reality differently from people who are not entrepreneurs. For example, why do some people decide to become entrepreneurs while others do not? Why do some people leave secure jobs and take risks and pursue a new lifestyle, such as starting a winery or art gallery? The answer to these questions lies in the mindset.

Many societies encourage entrepreneurs and consider entrepreneurship essential for the economic growth of a nation. Entrepreneurship is not limited to capitalist societies, as we also find entrepreneurs in communist countries such as Cuba, Vietnam, and China. In fact, entrepreneurship has a vital role to play in building national wealth. However, entrepreneurship may be difficult in some places, such as North Korea, where entrepreneurship may be seen as a threat.

Finally, we want to make it clear that entrepreneurship can happen to anyone who is willing to put in the time and energy. Entrepreneurs can be both men and women, they can be from every ethnicity and cultural background. Age, gender, or geographic location are no barriers to entrepreneurship. The decision to become an entrepreneur starts with mindset, and this mindset is the first and most important step towards entrepreneurship.

The most important factor for entrepreneurial success is mindset. For example, take the story of a 57-year-old woman who lost everything after her divorce, but built a multi-million dollar business from photos of her dog. The deciding factor in this story was her mindset.

# DEFINING ENTREPRENEURSHIP?

Although we have already used the terms entrepreneur and entrepreneurship, we have not yet defined what we mean by these terms. To do so, the reader must allow us to delve for another moment into the academic discussions that we think will ultimately be informative. One reason we find the stories about various entrepreneurs so interesting is that many believe these stories reflect a complex set of interrelated phenomena. Establishing entrepreneurship as a single scholarly field is nearly impossible. Still, for as long as entrepreneurship has been recognized or existed as a field of research, many have tried. Despite many efforts, there is no single definition of entrepreneurship to date. If you have seven entrepreneurship professors in a room, you are likely to have seventeen definitions. People with a psychology background will have one (or two), those from sociology will have another, economists will have several, and then there are those from finance and management who have their own biases about the subject. Even accountants are involved in this area, which is good because many academics in this field sometimes confuse revenue with profit.

That said, there seems to be broad agreement that a commercial entrepreneur (as opposed to a social entrepreneur) is generally someone who exploits opportunities for the purpose of economic wealth creation.

This idea has existed for centuries, starting with Catilion in 1775. Over the years, different authors have used different descriptions, ranging from a risk taker exploiting opportunities (Catilion 1755; Knight 1921; and 1803), or more precisely as an opportunity creator/innovator (Schumpeter 1934) or as a cautious seeker of opportunities (Kirzner 1973; Mises 1951). In 1776, Edwin Smith actually viewed the entrepreneur as a capitalist (Laddstrom 2005). Again, there is still little consensus in the field on how to study how opportunities are created or exploited.

# OPPORTUNITY RECOGNITION

However, a common understanding is that opportunity exists when there are competitive imperfections in the market (Venkataraman 1997). While Schumpeter (1934) and Kirzer (1973) clearly recognized that opportunity is at the core of entrepreneurship, they had different views on how opportunity and entrepreneurship are connected. Kirzner's (1973) entrepreneur is alert, finds some imbalance (flaw) in the market, and seeks equilibrium through entrepreneurship. Kirzner's entrepreneur does not need to create something new, but must be able to recognize and exploit what already exists. In other words, imitation is okay. In other words, Schumpeter's entrepreneur is at the edge of the production curve and seeks to push the curve outward, thereby creating individual and societal economic wealth. Kirzner's entrepreneur is inside the curve and attempts to reach the edge of the production curve through entrepreneurship (Landstrom 2005). We will discuss opportunity recognition in more detail later in this book. The important point here is how stories in the media conveniently ignore these theoretical gaps, but they are there when we look at cutting edge technology firms and firms operating in more traditional industrial sectors.

Academics love to debate in this tradition whether the chicken came or the egg. This is played out in academic circles with the debate over whether opportunities exist for everyone to discover and then exploit, or whether opportunities are created by the entrepreneur (Alvarez and Barney 2013). In the first case, the existence of opportunities is taken as a given and how opportunities are created has no bearing on how entrepreneurs exploit them. The latter is a more recent realization that opportunities can be created in many different ways and that the creation process can actually influence the process by which opportunities are exploited.

However, the practical implications of these differences are important. One view says that if anyone is alert, he or she can see an opportunity. The other view considers opportunity to be unique to the individual. It is possible that both are true, but the opportunities are different. We hope we haven't bored you with this academic discussion, but we think that too often the popular press has a tendency to think that all entrepreneurs are the same and yet the research suggests otherwise.

An interesting description of the approach to life and the search for opportunity is offered by Birch (1987; 91):

America is a nation of immigrants, but this does not mean that we are a mixture of Europe and Africa – and, increasingly, of Latin America and the Orient. Rather, this country has always attracted dissidents who were frustrated by feudal restrictions in the 18th century and the lack of economic and religious freedom and opportunity in their old countries in the 19th and 20th centuries.

Wariness to government restrictions on these freedoms and opportunities can be traced back to the colonial reluctance to follow British imperial policy, which led to revolution. Some have argued that this mixed approach to the United States is the reason that Americans are so entrepreneurial compared to more homogenous countries such as Japan. Clearly context and culture play a role in how goals are expressed. In this book we have made every effort to showcase examples of entrepreneurs from around the world whom we have worked with or are acquainted with.

# ENTREPRENEURIAL GOALS

Some scholars argue that the ultimate goal of entrepreneurship is to create wealth, and if wealth is not created, it is something different from entrepreneurship. The implication is that wealth creation is trumped by success. With this position we have some fundamental difficulties because wealth cannot be a primary or secondary goal, but rather it is simply a consequence of achieving some other goal. Dr. Jonas Salk could have patented his polio vaccine, but he chose to eradicate the disease instead. To say that you have to be rich to be considered an entrepreneur is ridiculous.

But, if you say that the only goal of entrepreneurs is wealth creation, there is another difficulty, because that means entrepreneurs are entrepreneurs only if they succeed (in wealth creation). That would mean that those who fail are not entrepreneurs. They are something else. Stories of unsuccessful entrepreneurs rarely make it into media narratives, somehow suggesting that failures are less frequent than successes. Yet we know that is not the case. If the twin brothers Frenchman Edgar Stanley and Freelan Oscar Stanley, who founded the Motor Carriage Company, had been successful, we would all be riding in steam cars. Failures happen, some more spectacular than others.

However, academic researchers have not really looked at unsuccessful entrepreneurs either. One reason for this is surely that it is very difficult to find entrepreneurs who are willing to talk about their failures. It is simply a very human thing. We prefer to talk about our successes rather than our failures. It is possible that there are many more factors at play in failure than in success. The reality is that we cannot really understand what is at play in success without looking at failure. This is where work done several years ago is very informative. There is evidence that entrepreneurs can start up to seven ventures in their lifetime and yet only one of them will be considered "successful." The issue is when does that successful attempt come? Does it happen early in this lifelong process or does it happen in the seventh attempt?

As another example, the problem with understanding bankruptcy statistics is not the attempt. The real issue is whether society, family, and your attitude will allow you to try again. One of our grandfathers once reminded us that you haven't really ridden a horse until you've been thrown off and put back on again. In many ways, entrepreneurship is really like riding a horse, a big, prancing horse.

# DIFFERENT GOALS FOR DIFFERENT PEOPLE

Then there is the fact that an entrepreneur may be involved for reasons entirely different than making money. Creating a business may be driven by the mere need to make ends meet or feed a family (an entrepreneurial need), think of our Persian Jews mentioned earlier. The purpose of becoming an entrepreneur may be to generate collective wealth—social wealth—the idea of doing good for someone else. In fact, in some cultures individual entrepreneurship is frowned upon because if you fail you may endanger the survival of your family or community. Thus, entrepreneurship becomes a community decision and activity.

There is also the reality that for personal reasons, such as increased quality of life (a very subjective definition), an individual may pursue a lifestyle form of entrepreneurship that is different from those focused on making a lot of money. Perhaps it is a desire to be able to stay in their rural hometown rather than moving to a big city? Perhaps it's the desire to turn a hobby into a life, for example, a person who is passionate about surfing or downhill skiing decides to open a store specializing in surfboards, snowboards and downhill skis? Perhaps it's the desire to cure an illness, certainly a noble goal. The issue is whether setting goals really defines success, but more on that later in this book. Throughout this book we give small examples and case studies of different types of entrepreneurs to demonstrate that entrepreneurs come from all genders, races, ethnic groups, nationalities and ages. What makes a business successful for us is the attitude, part of an entrepreneurial mindset.

# OTHER DEFINITIONAL ISSUES

There is another way to approach this definitional issue of entrepreneurship, and that is to try to define what entrepreneurship is not. However, this approach is not very helpful either. However, some of our colleagues are on the verge of describing entrepreneurship as something truly extraordinary, arguing that entrepreneurship means building high-growth firms.

We address the issue of growth in a later chapter of this book. However, for a more in-depth discussion of why this is a fool's errand, we refer you to our book Understanding the Myth of High Growth Firms: The Theory of the Greater Fool (Branbank et al. 2014).

Similarly, some consider second-generation family business owners not to be entrepreneurs, because they did not create the enterprise but inherited the firm. If that is the case, then Ray Kroc was not an entrepreneur at McDonald's, and neither were the McDonald brothers Richard and Mau-Rice, but their father Patrick was. This definition would mean that only founders can be entrepreneurs. Like McDonald's, where later arrivals would be acknowledged entrepreneurs, we have many examples of family firms that continue to be entrepreneurial from generation to generation, as seen in firms that reinvent themselves with new products, markets, and organizational structures. Heineken Brewing is another example of a family firm that is pursuing entrepreneurship in new markets and brands under the leadership of Alfred "Fred-Die" Heineken, the founder's grandson. Going back to necessity, entrepreneurs such as immigrants or oppressed minorities did not initially see any opportunities, but had to find a way to make a living and so they had to do something.

To say that this is not entrepreneurship is to deny the struggle of many of these people. Interestingly, many necessity-based firms are actually exploiting opportunities and the distinction between these types may be fuzzy at best.

Some people think that only those who have frame-breaking technology can be entrepreneurs. We strongly disagree. These technology entrepreneurs, who are really special cases, face completely different challenges than many "ordinary" entrepreneurs in established industries or necessity entrepreneurs trying to survive in physical form. They need a lot of initial funding and take forever to make a profit, if they ever manage to do so. Biotechnology entrepreneurs are a special case of technology entrepreneurs because it is about developing first the science, then the technology and only then finding out if there is a business opportunity involved. Perhaps, one thing common in all of the above is hard work and desire to achieve the goals which are different. If you think that becoming an entrepreneur is easy, then this is not the right career choice for you.

# SELF EMPLOYED ENTREPRENEURS

Recently, the U.S. Census Bureau estimated that the number of home-based businesses with no employees grew 23% over 10 years to a total of more than 23 million. Nationally, the revenue of these no-employee businesses has grown to more than $1.05 trillion.

It should be clear at this point that we take a broad and inclusive view of entrepreneurship. We think there is benefit to entrepreneurs taking this "big tent" approach. Take, for example, creative people or artists who sell their arts and crafts. In many cases those processes involve very little new technology, just paint, clay, metal and chaos.

However, as you will find, the Internet and digital technology are rapidly transforming the visual arts, as seen in the use of Photoshop software or 3D printing. The same can be said for musicians and performance artists, who have embraced new technologies in the creation of their art.

The point is that many self-employed people are actually people who are creating something, not just art, but also new technologies like software applications for cell phones. Typically, non-employer businesses are one-person businesses, such as a freelance designer. We all have people we know who do this and that on the side and friends who blog and sometimes earn income from advertising on the site. Then there are YouTube sensations who give advice on various topics and eventually gain a large following. We've seen the same thing happen with Twitter; users earn money because of their posts. Sometimes these ventures involve family members and friends who are not paid. These are examples we can all relate to, where the venture is the entrepreneur's primary source of income. Just think of the real estate agents you know, or even your personal medical doctor. In other cases, solopreneurs may operate their venture as a side job. If you're a parent, you know these people because they provide childcare and tutoring for your children.

# REFERENCE FOR SELF-EMPLOYED ENTREPRENEURS

Cities are often evaluated on viability – not just technology and manufacturing firms – but on quality of life, including the arts. Where would New Orleans be without the music and culinary entrepreneurs who have made the city as famous for its food as it is for its music and nightlife? Many self-employed people are often not considered by the media and policymakers as demanding of attention. Their value has often been overlooked. What brought New Orleans back to life after Hurricane Katrina was the vibrancy of the art, music and food scenes. Had they left, the city would have turned into a ghost town with rickety buildings.
However, recently cities like New Orleans and Austin have seen as much value in promoting their artists as their technology firms or oil firms. Just look at Austin, Texas, which bills itself as the "live music capital of the world" and hosts the SXSW (South by Southwest) festival that brings together technology, music, and film. In Austin alone, for example, one of the fastest growing self-employment sectors is the arts, entertainment, and recreation sector. In 2003, there were 5,931 such enterprises. By 2013, the number of such firms had grown to 11,355, an increase of 91%,

with estimated revenues of $271 million in 2013. This is no small part of the economic life of a city like Austin. One such non-employee enterprise in the arts sector is run by Austin-area artist Danny Babinas. His current paintings focus on animal subjects. He commissions portraits of people's pets, Texas' ubiquitous longhorn cattle, as well as endangered species such as elephants and rhinos (see Figures 1.3 and 1.4). He has sold his paintings not only in Austin but around the world; thanks to the Internet, which allows him to be free to travel to art shows and exhibit in galleries, saving him the associated overhead costs.

Using PayPal, he is able to take payments by credit card. The following is an example of some of his art:
Historically, one only needs to look at artists like Rembrandt Harmenszoon van Rijn, the father of the "selfie", Paulo Picasso, Andy Warhol, George F. Handel, Richard Wagner or the Beatles collectively, or Lennon and McCartney individually, to see that all were successful on many dimensions, including financial. All had a huge impact on society. Warhol's print runs became instant production lines. Picasso outsourced his ceramics to a family firm for production. Lennon and McCartney created an entire industry that had a lasting impact on society and music. One can look at Taylor Swift's current success. It is clear that her current musical and business skills are only an indication of what her entrepreneurial talents will yield in the future.

DREAM TO REALITY

51

# A FALSE DUALISM

If you recall, we previously discussed the work of David Birch and the role of small business and entrepreneurs. At this point we perhaps need to consider these terms in a little more detail. Many of the early scholars who argued that small business owners are not entrepreneurs (e.g., Carland et al. 1984) had no real understanding of how small firms operate. These researchers failed to appreciate the innovations often created by these firms, nor how much an entrepreneur's personality affects their operations (think Donald Trump here). Reading their definitions of a small business owner and an entrepreneur 30 years ago today is more confusing than helpful. Consider the following (Carland et al. 1984; 358)-

A small business owner is a person who establishes and manages a business with the primary objective of pursuing personal goals. The business should be the primary source of income and will consume the majority of the individual's time and resources. The owner views the business as an extension of his or her personality, intricately linked to family needs and desires.
An entrepreneur is a person who establishes and manages a business with the primary objective of generating profit and growth. An entrepreneur is primarily characterized by innovative behavior and adopting strategic management practices in business.

The same article also distinguishes a small business enterprise from an entrepreneurial venture:

A small business enterprise is a business that is independently owned and operated, that does not dominate a sector, and that does not engage in any new marketing or innovative practices.
An entrepreneurial enterprise is one that engages in at least one of Schumpeter's four categories of behavior: that is, the primary goals of an entrepreneurial enterprise are profitability and growth and the business is characterized by innovative practices.

Finally, the Carland article summarizes a review of the literature between 1848 (Mill) and 1982 (Dunkelberg and Kapur), which described characteristics that describe entrepreneurs, but not explicitly small business owners. Birth order, sex, or marital status were excluded, "because a potential entrepreneur is unable to change those variables to increase his or her chances of success." These characteristics that characterize an entrepreneur include risk bearing, source of formal authority, innovation, desire for responsibility, risk aversion, moderate risk taker, need for achievement, ambition, desire for independence, drive, technical knowledge, communication ability, autonomy, aggressiveness, strength, recognition, need for power, internal locus of control, personal value orientation, self-confidence, goal orientation, creativity, energetic, positive response to failure, independence oriented, and craftsman oriented. The implication was that entrepreneurs were male and Anglo-Saxon in ethnicity. Carlton's article is a good example of how people's perceptions and understanding of who an entrepreneur is, what entrepreneurial characteristics are, and what entrepreneurship is all about have changed over the past three decades. Certainly, small business owners also seek profitability and growth. Frankly, the description of a small business owner sounds very similar to the description of many entrepreneurs today, as portrayed by the mass media, which makes an entrepreneur essentially a small business owner as well. The previous list of characteristics makes almost everyone an entrepreneur. These characteristics can also be found in small business owners or anyone else who is not an entrepreneur, but who is successful in their profession or career.

# DO THE GOALS DIFFER?

We strongly question the fundamental assumption that the primary goals of an entrepreneurial venture are profitability and growth. We believe that these can be achieved by doing something else well and that they are consequences of achieving those goals. For some people, money may be the primary goal, but not always. If money is the only goal, one is reminded of the response of Jesse James, the famous hero of the Wild West in the United States in the 1800s, when asked why he robbed banks: "It's the money." We are not suggesting that bank robbery is a crime. In entrepreneurial terms, it is a difficult task, but certainly one might think it is much easier than starting a company and waiting for years for revenues or profits to come in. If earning profits is the goal, many firms that would be considered entrepreneurial would fall out of the category of entrepreneurship. Most Kirznerian entrepreneurs would be defined as small business owners. If we took these definitions and applied them to today's world, we would have trouble defining Twitter founder Jack Dorsey as an entrepreneur (although many would certainly see him as an entrepreneur – and a successful one).

Consider this quote from an article published in Newsweek on October 20, 2008-

Consider that Twitter, a "micro-blogging" site launched in 2006, raised a reported $15 million in venture funding earlier this year at an undisclosed valuation — even though the company hasn't made a dime yet and its executives aren't trying. "We're in a pre-revenue phase. Our focus is on growth."

Yet, we know that when this founder sold Twitter, he became a billionaire. The goal was obviously not to make a profit for the firm, but to increase its valuation so that the owner could exit and create his own wealth, i.e., personal profit. Perhaps it is a legal form of bank robbery.

It should be clear at this point that defining entrepreneurship or entrepreneurship is not an easy task. It should also be clear that we question the very need for economic wealth creation as the primary goal. For example, Johannisson (2005) views entrepreneurship as existentially motivated. That is, entrepreneurship is seen as a way of life that involves a full commitment by the individual. Perhaps this could explain entrepreneurs who start up to seven business ventures in a lifetime. This brings to mind other possible goals and desires that are involved in entrepreneurship, as we discussed in Carsrud and Brånbank (2011). In other words, goals are an important part of entrepreneurial motivation.

# A MINI-CASE EXAMPLE

For an example of a motivated entrepreneur, let's look at Patrick Dupre Quigley, another Florida social entrepreneur we know well.

Patrick trained as a classical musician at the University of Notre Dame and later Yale University. He has worked closely with many. Michael Tilson Thomas was a renowned conductor. Interestingly, he had also worked at several marketing and public relations firms while in school and knew there had to be a way to make classical music accessible. He had a clear goal: to create a sustainable classical music group in the South Florida market. Despite Miami having a new and spectacular concert hall and a state-of-the-art opera/ballet house, he had seen many of its classical music groups struggle and/or fail like the Florida Philharmonic.

Patrick also realized that young audiences were not interested in classical concerts longer than ninety minutes, and the costs of such organizations could not be covered by the traditional model of concert revenue and donations. He also realized that young audiences would not sit through a ninety-minute classical concert. He also knew there were many fine independent musicians, especially singers, whom he could bring in, pay well for a particular concert, and that once the concert was over they would go home or move on to the next gig. The result of his efforts is Seraphic Fire and its associated orchestra, one of Florida's few profitable nonprofit arts organizations.

We look at this example as an example of how a clear goal can motivate an entrepreneur, in this case a social entrepreneur in the arts sector. The point is that Patrick saw a need and created a goal to meet that need. The result has been pure joy for those of us who have attended his concerts, or bought CDs, or downloaded music performed by his groups.

# OPPORTUNITIES & ENTREPRENEURSHIP

Most researchers would agree that no matter what the individual is motivated by, or what the form of entrepreneurship is, the existence of an opportunity is a fundamental requirement, even if the entrepreneur is doing business out of necessity. The person intending to become an entrepreneur must somehow perceive that the opportunity exists. Whether that opportunity is viable as a basis for venture creation is an entirely different issue. In fact, the person who sees the opportunity must perceive that it is a good opportunity. To reflect this reality, we have used over the years a definition of entrepreneurship that was originally proposed by two people.

The definition proposed by Harvard Enterprise School colleagues, Stevenson and Jarillo (1990), seems to us to be the most appropriate. This definition is also useful for necessity entrepreneurs (who are forced to find opportunities). Also important is that it allows both Kirzner's and Schumpeter's entrepreneurs to exist. This definition was originally-

Entrepreneurship is the process by which individuals – whether individually or within organizations – pursue opportunities regardless of the resources they currently control.

While this may not be a great operational definition for scientific research purposes, it does allow us to cast a wide net over who an entrepreneur is. It allows us to see how stories about entrepreneurs reflect this definition across new firms, existing family firms, and even large, multinational corporations.

# PRACTICE

Based on your reading, discuss opportunity discovery and opportunity creation in class. What is the difference? Think about entrepreneurs you know personally. How did they discover or create their opportunity? Did they prepare a business plan or did they have a plan in mind that was not formally written down? Did they have to revise the plan, how often, and what were the reasons for revision? Did they consider the possibility of failure?

Was there anything they overlooked in the process of creating the firm? What was the biggest surprise?

# WHAT IS IT TO BE SUCCESSFUL?

The meaning of success is different for every person. Some measure it in money, some in happiness and satisfaction. Meaning, success is not bound by a fixed definition. It depends on what you give importance to in your life. Some people believe that if they have a lot of money, a big house, and luxury cars, then they are successful. At the same time, some people believe that if they find peace, satisfaction, and happiness in their life, then this is their success.

Now let us understand this with the example of a great entrepreneur Ratan Tata.

Ratan Tata's name is taken with great respect and honor in the business world. He took the Tata Group to new heights and started many successful business ventures. But for him success did not mean just making profits. He always gave priority to the well-being of the employees of his companies and service to the society.

A great example from Ratan Tata's life is when he launched Tata Nano. At that time there were many middle class families in India who traveled on bikes and buying a car was a dream for them. Ratan Tata understood the need of these families and decided to make a car that was affordable and safe. He considered the well-being of these families as his success rather than big profits. The purpose of Tata Nano was to give an opportunity to even a common man to fulfill his dream of owning four wheels.

Ratan Tata believed that true success is when your achievements benefit society, and you can make someone's life better. This is why he always kept ethics and humanity at the top in his business. Whether it is about the rights of employees or environmental protection, Ratan Tata always considered social responsibility as a measure of his success.

His approach teaches us that success should not be limited to money only. The true meaning of success is to bring positive change in the lives of others, make the world around you better, and stand by your values.

This example makes it clear that there is no one fixed measure of success. It completely depends on the person what he considers important in life.

# WHY CHECK FOR SUCCESS?

Success does not mean just winning or achieving a goal. Real success is when we understand it deeply, examine it, and find out whether we took steps in the right direction or not. Often people stop after success and think that they have achieved everything, but if success is not examined, the chances of making mistakes in the future increase.

Examining success helps us understand which step made us successful, what can be improved, and what strategy should be adopted for the future. This helps us to become better and motivates us to remain successful in the long run.

Now let us understand this with the example of the education system of Finland and Sweden. These two countries are an example in front of the world in the field of education, but their success story is different. Let us understand this deeply.

In the early 1970s, Finland's education system had many problems. Their students were performing average in international examinations, and the country's leaders realized that education needed improvement. But instead of taking big steps without thinking, they first examined their current education system.

After this examination, Finland made many small but important reforms. They focused on improving the quality of teachers, gave them higher education, and took steps to make education a respectable profession. Apart from this, Finland decided to put less pressure on students. They made sure that children had real understanding instead of just memorizing.

Gradually, these reforms began to show results. Today, Finland's education system is considered one of the best in the world. This success was only possible because Finland examined its old system, understood what was wrong, and took small steps to improve it.

Sweden also took big steps to reform education in the 1990s. They moved towards privatizing education, so that there could be competition among schools and improvement could take place. Sweden's policy worked well in some schools, but overall the results were not as effective as Finland's.

Sweden did not examine its education system as deeply as Finland did. Privatization led to some schools performing well, but inequality increased in many schools, and the level of education declined. As a result, Sweden's education system did not reach the same heights in the world as Finland.

The example of Finland and Sweden teaches us an important lesson about why it is important to examine success. Finland examined its old education system deeply, made improvements, and today they are at the top in the field of education. On the other hand, Sweden took steps to improve education but did not pay enough attention to properly testing and understanding its success, which resulted in its reforms being ineffective.

This example teaches us that it is not enough to be successful, but it is also important to examine our success. This examination helps us understand what is the reason for our success, and what things we should focus on in the future.

By examining success, we not only improve our present but can also make better strategies for the future. When we analyze our success, we can learn from our mistakes and find a way not to repeat them in the future.

So, we should not stop even after success. We should make sure that we understand our success well, examine it, and always keep trying to improve ourselves.

# DEFINING SUCCESS

Success means different things to each individual. It can be an achievement in one area of life or an attempt to make life satisfying overall. Success is difficult to define because it cannot be measured only by wealth, fame, or heights reached. It requires a broader perspective that includes positive impact on society and individual life. To understand success better, we will look at some important examples from India and abroad, which show us the diversity and depth of success.

The role played by Mahatma Gandhi in the freedom struggle is one of the most important stories in Indian history. For him, success did not mean just independence, but moving society forward in the direction of morality and equality while remaining steadfast on the principles of truth and non-violence.

Gandhi's life shows that the measure of success is not just achieving a goal, but also the way in which you achieve it. He followed the principles of Satyagraha and non-violence and gave birth to a new political approach across the world. His success had an impact not only on India but also on other independence movements around the world.

While Mahatma Gandhi was a symbol of morality and social change, J.R.D. Tata became a symbol of the creation and development of Indian industry. As the chairman of the Tata Group, he took Indian industry to new heights.

J.R.D. Tata's success was not just in enterprise. He always insisted that the industry run by him should benefit not only the company but also the society. He made significant contributions in the field of employee welfare, education and health. Success for him meant being a responsible industrialist who thinks about the welfare of society and contributes to it.

Mother Teresa's life proves that success does not mean only economic or professional advancement. For her, the criterion of success was that she could serve the suffering and poor people. She devoted her entire life to serving the poor and sick people of Kolkata.

The symbol of Mother Teresa's success is that she set an example of service to humanity. Her selfless service earned her admiration and respect all over the world. Success for her meant helping others and improving their lives. This is a form of success that cannot be measured by material possessions or position, but is linked to the true spirit of humanity.

Ratan Tata, the former chairman of the Tata Group, is known not only as a successful industrialist but also as an ethical and responsible business leader. For him, success did not just mean making profits, but he ensured that his business had a positive impact on society and the environment.

Under his leadership, the Tata Group launched several important projects that were dedicated to the betterment of society. For example, the Tata Nano was introduced as a car that the common man could afford. Ratan Tata believed that success is complete only when you are also working for the betterment of society. His success story shows that business success can also be combined with social responsibility and ethics.

Ila Bhatt is an Indian social worker and a prominent leader of the cooperative movement. She founded the Self-Employed Women's Association (SEWA), which works to provide employment and empowerment to women workers. For her, success meant empowering poor and unorganized women economically and giving them respect and rights.

Ila Bhatt's measure of success is not just the economic prosperity of the organization she founded, but the fact that her efforts have made millions of women self-reliant. Her success shows that social change and empowerment can also be an important aspect of success.

Elon Musk, founder of companies like SpaceX and Tesla, creates a new definition of success. For him, success does not mean just making money, but facing and solving the world's biggest challenges.

Through SpaceX, Musk has taken significant steps towards making space travel affordable and accessible, and through Tesla, he revolutionized the world of electric vehicles. Musk believes that his measure of success will be that he can lead humanity to a better future, which includes clean energy and life in space. His success story shows that dreaming big and having the passion to fulfill them can also be a form of success.

Former Japanese Prime Minister Shinzo Abe's success can be measured by his contribution to economic and political reforms. He implemented an economic policy called "Abenomics", which aimed to revive Japan's slowing economy.

For Shinzo Abe, success meant that his policies brought employment, investment, and economic stability to the country. His political successes not only helped improve Japan's economic condition but also established him as an important global leader. This shows that success is not just limited to personal achievement, but also includes work done for the country and society.

Malala Yousafzai, a young education activist from Pakistan, fought for the right to education for girls. She was shot by the Taliban, but she did not give up. She continued her fight for education with even more vigor and today she has become a symbol of girls' education around the world.

For Malala, success was not just about completing her education, but about ensuring that girls around the world have the right to education. Her measure of success is that she has spread awareness about education not only in her country but around the world and has become an inspiration to millions of children.

There is no single measure of success. It depends on the individual's attitude, goals, and responsibilities. The stories of great people like Mahatma Gandhi, Mother Teresa, J.R.D. Tata, Ratan Tata, Elon Musk, and Malala Yousafzai show that success is not just about personal achievements, but about having a positive impact on society and the world.

True success is when the hard work you put in and your principles make the world a better place. Whether it's spreading education, eradicating poverty, or innovating technology—the true measure of success is how your actions affect the lives of others.

# DEFINING FAILURE

Failure does not only mean failure or not being able to achieve success in something. It is an experience that makes us realize the mistakes and weaknesses in our goals and efforts. If failure is understood correctly, it can become an important learning that helps to succeed in the future. In fact, behind any great success lies the story of one or more failures. Failure not only makes us aware of our limitations, but it also provides an opportunity to reshape and improve our efforts.

In 2019, India attempted to land on the surface of the Moon through the Chandrayaan-2 mission. ISRO scientists had worked on this mission for years, and it was a historic moment for India. But at the last moment, Vikram Lander lost contact and the mission was considered unsuccessful.

This failure definitely discouraged the scientific community of India, but ISRO did not consider it the end of its efforts. They learned from their mistakes and planned a new mission in the form of Chandrayaan-3, which successfully landed on the surface of the Moon in 2023. The failure of Chandrayaan-2 made ISRO even stronger and proved that facing failure can be an important step towards growth.

Thomas Edison is known worldwide for his invention of the bulb, but very few people know that he faced failures thousands of times before making this invention successful. Edison himself said, "I have not failed, I have just found 10,000 ways that don't work."

This thinking of his shows that failure is only a temporary condition. Instead of giving up on failure, he tried again and again and finally he succeeded. His failure motivated him to search for new ways and this failure led to his success.

Japan faced the "Lost Decade" in the 1990s, when their economy went into a severe recession. This was a big failure for Japan, because till the 1980s it was one of the fastest growing economies in the world.

But Japan learned from this economic failure and changed its policies. They emphasized on technological development, innovation, and social security and gradually revived their economy. This failure gave Japan an opportunity to understand that constant improvement and adaptation is necessary to keep the economy stable and prosperous.

Failure is an inevitable and important part of life, which is often seen from a negative perspective. But, in reality, failure does not only make us feel failure, but it is also a process of deep learning and growth. It is an experience that gives us an opportunity to discover our mistakes and weaknesses, and motivates us to work even harder towards our goals.

The road to success is not always smooth and straight. It often has many twists and turns, with failure being a key element. When we face failures, it gives us an opportunity to recognize our true potential and provides us with an opportunity to improve our strategies and approach. Failure is a teacher that teaches us patience, resilience, and the art of problem solving.

The real value of failure is understood when we start looking at it as an opportunity rather than an obstacle. It gives us an opportunity to improve and change our actions. The learnings from the experience of failure help us adopt new strategies and achieve better results in the future.

True success is achieved when we accept the experience of failure, understand it and move forward by learning from it. Without failure, we can never recognize our true potential and use our full abilities.

Thus, failure is only a temporary situation that helps us take an important step forward towards success. It teaches us that despite failures, we should continue our journey and never give up.

In fact, looking at failure from the right perspective and learning from it, paves the way for us to achieve success in various spheres of life. It reminds us that true success does not mean only achieving the goal, but also maintaining faith in your efforts and dreams despite failures.

# MEASUREMENT ISSUES IN DEFINING SUCCESS/FAILURE

Measurement issues in defining success and failure are often complex because these concepts are highly personal and relative. There is no single universal criterion or tool for measuring success and failure; instead, they vary depending on different perspectives, standards, and contexts. Here we will discuss the major problems in measuring success and failure:

The definition of success and failure depends on the individual's perspective and the standards of society. Success for one person may mean a high salary, while for another it may mean a satisfactory quality of life, family well-being, or contribution to society. Similarly, the criteria for failure may also be personal—such as falling behind in one's career or not being able to meet one's personal goals. This diversity makes measuring success and failure difficult because standards vary.

To measure success and failure, clarity of objectives and goals is extremely important. When the individual or organization has clear and measurable goals, measuring success and failure is easier. For example, for a business company, meeting sales goals or making a profit may be clear indicators. But if there is ambiguity or uncertainty in the goals, measuring success and failure becomes difficult.

Success and failure can be measured by numerical parameters, such as revenue, profit, or marks in exams. But sometimes success and failure depend on qualitative elements, such as personal satisfaction, mental peace, or positive impact in society. Qualitative elements are difficult to measure and their evaluation depends on personal experience and emotional attitude.

While measuring success and failure, one also has to take into account the long-term and immediate perspective. A person or organization may fail to achieve immediate goals, but achieve success from a long-term perspective. For example, starting a new business may be an initial failure, but with time and experience the business may become successful. Therefore, it is important to understand success and failure from a long-term perspective.

India's Chandrayaan-2 mission is a prime example. The mission's objective was to land on the surface of the Moon and collect data. Initially, the mission's Vikram lander lost contact, due to which it was considered a failure. However, despite this failure, ISRO continued to make efforts to fulfill its objective and successfully landed on the surface of the moon through Chandrayaan-3. The standard of measurement here was clear goals and long-term vision, which ultimately paved the way towards success.

In the Indian education system, success and failure are often measured only in terms of test scores. A student who scores high in a test is considered successful, while one who scores low is considered unsuccessful. But, in real life, this standard does not reflect success in its entirety. Personal growth, skills, and experiences are also important, which go beyond test scores.

The definition and criteria of success and failure are complex and multifaceted. They are not limited to numerical figures, but also depend on personal standards, cultural contexts, and long-term perspectives.

Quantitative criteria such as financial gains, test scores, or professional achievements are often used to measure success. However, these criteria represent only one aspect. Personal satisfaction, quality of life, and contribution to society also play an important role in real success.

Evaluating failure is equally complex. Failures are often viewed from an immediate perspective, while it is important to recognize long-term improvement and growth. Sometimes immediate failure is an important step towards long-term success.

To understand success and failure, we need to take into account a variety of perspectives. Personal standards, external and internal factors, cultural differences, and long-term perspectives all influence these concepts.

Ultimately, measuring success and failure on a concrete yardstick can be challenging. But proper understanding and evaluation of these can help us not only learn from our failures but also understand our successes in a more concrete way. This helps us to improve our efforts and face life's challenges.

Both success and failure are integral parts of life, which guide us towards growth and improvement. Their proper recognition and understanding makes the journey of life more meaningful and inspiring.

# SUCCESS IN AN ENTREPRENEURIAL CONTEXT

Entrepreneurial success is not limited to economic profits, market position, or technological achievements. It is a complex process that involves many factors such as innovation, organizational strategy, long-term vision, and social impact. Through the following examples, we can understand how success in the entrepreneurial context can be measured from different aspects.

Elon Musk founded SpaceX in 2002, which has become a major player in space exploration and technology. Initially, SpaceX faced many failures. Rocket launches failed in 2006, 2007, and 2008, putting the company's financial situation in crisis. Despite these failures, Musk never gave up and constantly improved the company's strategies.

In 2015, SpaceX launched the world's first reusable rocket. This reduced the cost of space travel and set a new standard for many other companies.

In 2020, SpaceX launched the first prototype of its Starship, a crucial step towards future human missions to Mars.

In 2021, SpaceX completed its funding round with a valuation of $74 billion, making it one of the most valuable private companies in the world.

There are many parameters to define success in the context of entrepreneurship that are not limited to just financial gains. Elements such as innovation, long-term vision, marketing, branding, and global expansion also play an important role. Examples of the world's leading entrepreneurs and companies show that entrepreneurial success is a complex and multifaceted process, in which continuous effort, strategic thinking, and innovation play an important role. These examples make us understand that achieving success requires focusing not only on immediate gains but also on long-term planning and growth. The ability to face challenging situations and having a clear vision are extremely important to succeed in the entrepreneurial journey.

# IN-DEPTH ANALYSIS OF FIRM FOUNDING SUCCESS

Defining success can be as personal and varied as the path to achieving it. For different entrepreneurs, success can mean different things – for some it may be financial gain, for others it may be innovation, social impact, or personal satisfaction.

Bill Gates founded Microsoft in 1975 with Paul Allen. At that time, the computer industry was still in its infancy. Gates dreamed of every home having a personal computer. He made operating systems and software widely accessible, making Microsoft a global force. The Windows operating system made it easier to operate computers around the world, and established Gates as a successful entrepreneur.

Success for Bill Gates was not limited to just growing Microsoft. Once the company achieved global success, Gates turned his attention to social service. He founded the Bill & Melinda Gates Foundation in 2000, with the goal of improving healthcare and promoting education around the world. Gates has donated a large portion of his wealth to philanthropy, making it clear that for him success also means giving back to society.

Reed Hastings co-founded Netflix in 1997, which was initially a DVD rental service. But he quickly saw that internet streaming could become the entertainment medium of the future. He changed his company's entire strategy and in 2010 Netflix launched streaming services. It was a risky move, but it made the company the world's largest streaming service, completely changing the way traditional TV and movies were watched.

Success for Reed Hastings meant adapting and innovating with the times. He saw how technological advancements could completely transform businesses, and he took full advantage of it. For him, success meant that his company was always future-ready and could understand the changing requirements of the audience.

Ratan Tata took over the reins of the Tata Group in 1991 and made the company an iconic brand globally. Under his leadership, the Tata Group made several international acquisitions, such as Jaguar-Land Rover and Corus. Apart from this, he focused towards social innovation and launched projects like Tata Nano, which made the dream of owning a car a reality for the common man.

Ratan Tata has always said that success for him means having a positive impact on society. Through its social and economic programs, the Tata Group has shown that a business is not just for profits, but also for serving the society. Ratan Tata said that he sees his business as a means to bring change in society.

This story teaches us that success is not just a set criterion, but it is linked to personal attitude and different aspects of life. Every entrepreneur's definition of success depends on their values, goals and social responsibilities.

The conclusion of this story is that defining success is as personal as the path to achieve it. For some, success may mean economic prosperity, for others innovation and adaptation. At the same time, for some, success may mean giving back to society and bringing change in society.

Real success is when your achievements benefit not only you, but also society and the world. We must understand that the definition of success cannot be one-dimensional, but it is made up of many aspects. Whether it's personal satisfaction, social service, or innovation and adaptation – the true measure of success is how you can improve the world with your efforts.

# COMPREHENSIVE APPROACH

Over the past decade, many startup companies have achieved "unicorn" status. Unicorns are companies with a valuation of more than $1 billion. For example, companies like Airbnb, Uber, and WeWork expanded their services worldwide and brought about major changes in the tech industry. These companies have redefined new business models, emerging technologies, and consumer experiences.

According to researchers, the success of unicorn companies should not be measured only by their valuation or profitability, but by their innovation capability, consumer satisfaction, and long-term sustainability. Airbnb transformed the hospitality industry and gave consumers a new experience. Uber changed the way of transportation, but its work culture and legal challenges also need attention.

Muhammad Yunus founded Grameen Bank in Bangladesh in 1983 with the aim of providing small loans to poor and underprivileged people. This bank helped millions of people to become self-reliant and played a vital role in poverty alleviation. It was a unique model that empowered economically weaker sections.

Entrepreneurship researchers consider this type of social enterprises as a successful model. The success of Grameen Bank is based on the fact that it did not only aim to make profits but also helped the underprivileged sections of society. It proved that a business can also have a social impact and contribute to economic development.

The view of entrepreneurship researchers clearly shows that success should be viewed from a broader perspective. Profits, innovation, social impact, and environmental sustainability – all these are important aspects of success.

These events teach that success should not be limited to the financial perspective. Real success is when you not only grow your business but also make a positive contribution to society, environment, and humanity. The real criterion for entrepreneurship should be that you can make the world a better place through your efforts.

# ANCIENT STORY OF SUCCESS

In ancient tales, the path to success is often explained through patience, perseverance, and hard work. One such famous tale is that of Sisyphus, which symbolizes the constant struggle to achieve success in Greek mythology. Sisyphus was tasked with carrying a stone to the top of a hill, but every time the stone reached the top, the stone would fall down again. This tale teaches us that the path to success is not always easy, and for this we have to try again and again.

This ancient tale also teaches us some modern events, which prove that success is not just a final destination, but a continuous journey.

The journey of James Dyson, who founded the Dyson company, was also similar to the tale of Sisyphus. Dyson invented the bagless vacuum cleaner, but it took him 15 years and 5,126 failed prototypes to bring it to the market. No company was accepting his invention, but he did not give up. Eventually she started her own company and today Dyson has become a global brand.

J.K. Rowling's story is also similar to the ancient legend of Sisyphus. Before becoming the author of Harry Potter, Rowling was struggling with poverty and her novel was rejected by 12 publishers. But she did not give up and eventually her series of books gained worldwide fame. Today, Harry Potter is one of the most successful literary works in the world.

The main message of the ancient tale of Sisyphus is that patience and persistence play an extremely important role in the path of success. Sisyphus tries to reach the top of the hill every time, even if the stone falls down again. Similarly, James Dyson and J.K. Rowling also faced many failures in their lives, but they never gave up their efforts. This teaches us that the key to success is to keep trying despite failures.

The tale of Sisyphus and modern examples make it clear that failure is only a stop, not the end of the journey. Dyson made 5,126 failed prototypes, but he did not give up and eventually found success. Similarly, J.K. Rowling continued her writing despite many rejections and achieved success. This teaches us that failure should not be considered the final one, but it should be considered an opportunity to learn and try again.

The tale of Sisyphus also teaches us that determination and confidence are necessary to achieve success. No matter how many challenges come, the real success is to keep moving towards your goal. The stories of Dyson and Rolling also give the same message. They accepted their circumstances as a challenge and moved forward believing in their ability.

This story teaches us that success is a difficult and long journey that requires patience, continuous effort, perseverance, confidence, and innovation. No matter how many challenges come in life, real success is to have the courage to move forward without giving up on failures.

# SUCCESS AND OPPORTUNITIES

Success is not just about external achievements, but it is also about one's inner satisfaction, purposeful life and social contribution. The path to achieving it may vary for different individuals. For one person, success may mean earning a huge amount of money, while for someone else, it may be about living their passion and making the most of their skills. For some, it may be about bringing about a positive change in society.

Success should not be seen as just a final destination, but it is a process of continuous effort, learning and growth. It is also about the experiences that one gains in that process. Hence, the measurement of success is personal and practical—how it defines you, how you define it.

Opportunity is a situation or time when you get favorable conditions to achieve your goals. Opportunity is important only when it is recognized and acted upon at the right time. The ability to grab the right opportunity depends on your thinking, attitude and decision-making power. Many incidents in history show that even ordinary people can achieve extraordinary success by utilizing the opportunity in the right direction.

Identifying opportunities and capitalizing on them is not an easy task. Many times it comes in the form of challenges and struggles, which people ignore. But only those who are able to recognize the opportunities hidden in these challenges are able to make their place in history.

Amul (Anand Milk Union Limited) was founded in 1946, when the dairy industry of India lacked a cooperative model. At that time, small farmers and dairy producers were not able to get a fair price for their produce. This was a big problem, but Dr. Verghese Kurien saw an opportunity in this challenge. He laid the foundation of a cooperative dairy model, which had direct involvement of farmers.

Amul made India the largest milk producer in the world by innovating in milk production and marketing. Apart from this, Amul took its brand to the hearts of the people through several marketing campaigns. The advertising campaign of "Amul Girl" holds a unique place in the Indian advertising industry. Today, Amul has made its mark not only in India but also abroad.

For Dr. Kurien, success did not mean only profits, but it was linked to the social change he brought about in the economic condition of small farmers. His cooperative model made millions of farmers self-reliant and gave them a fair place in the market.

Amul's success teaches us that even a small opportunity, if identified and leveraged correctly, can transform not just an individual but an entire community. Dr. Verghese Kurien saw the challenge as an opportunity and acted upon it to establish a unique model that led to India's dairy revolution.

Jack Ma founded Alibaba in China in 1999, when China's internet market was very limited. Jack Ma faced many failures in the beginning, but he saw it as an opportunity. He connected small and medium traders to the global market by providing them an online platform. Today Alibaba is one of the world's largest e-commerce companies, and Jack Ma is counted among China's most successful entrepreneurs. This is the result of his vision and ability to recognize opportunities.

In the 1990s, India saw a significant opportunity to boost its IT industry. Policy reforms were made to take advantage of this opportunity, making India one of the largest IT services exporters in the world today. Companies like Tata Consultancy Services (TCS), Infosys, and Wipro capitalized on this opportunity and made their mark globally. This incident teaches us that a country can touch new heights of success by taking the right steps at the right time.

Success does not mean only external achievements; it is deeply connected with inner satisfaction, social contribution, and purpose in life. The definition of success may vary for every person, and the path to achieving it is also different. But what is common in all successes is the ability to identify and capitalize on opportunities.

Successful individuals and organizations throughout history have proven that opportunities are hidden in challenges. The stories of Jack Ma, Dr. Verghese Kurien, and India's IT industry teach us that success comes only to those who recognize the right opportunity at the right time and act on it.

Therefore, success should be seen as a journey, where every experience and every challenge brings a new opportunity. Patience, perseverance and innovation play an important role in this journey. If we develop the ability to recognize opportunities and use them in the right direction, we can achieve extraordinary success not only individually but also collectively.

# LINKING SUCCESS TO ENTREPRENEURIAL GOALS

There is a deep connection between success and entrepreneurship. Entrepreneurship is not just about starting a business, but taking concrete steps towards a successful and sustainable business. When we set our entrepreneurial goals in a clear and measurable way, the chances of success also increase.

Imagine Aditya, a young entrepreneur, decided to open a cafe. It was not enough for him to just open the cafe, but he set several important goals:

Aditya set a goal for his cafe to have 100 customers every day. Along with this, he ensured that every customer gets high quality service, so that they also come back and give positive reviews of the cafe. To achieve this goal, Aditya built a well-trained and motivated team in his cafe, which takes care of every need of the customers.

Aditya also set financial goals clearly. He set a target of reaching Rs 10 lakh in the sales of the cafe in the first year. After this, he set a target of increasing sales by 20% every year. To achieve this goal, Aditya created a solid financial plan and monitored it regularly. He prepared a budget keeping in mind the income and expenditure of his business and managed it properly.

Another important goal of Aditya was to buy fresh fruits and vegetables from local farmers. This would not only benefit his business but also provide financial support to the local farmers and boost the local economy. Aditya approached local markets and purchased fresh products from there, which benefited both parties.

Aditya took several steps to achieve his objectives. He designed a great marketing strategy for his cafe. He promoted his business using social media, local events, and discount offers. He made a good plan to bring the cafe's special menu items and offers to the people.

Apart from this, Aditya ensured that the services and products offered at the cafe were of high quality. He trained his team towards excellence in customer service. As a result, the cafe started getting positive reviews and customers remained satisfied.

Aditya built a strong foundation for his business and emerged as a successful entrepreneur. The clarity of his goals and the steps taken to achieve them ensured his success.

Linking success to entrepreneurial goals is only possible when you set clear and measurable goals for your business and create a solid and well-thought-out plan to achieve those goals.

Entrepreneurship, the journey of starting a new business and making it successful, is inherently full of challenges. To be successful in this journey, first of all, you must clearly define your goals. Clear goals mean that you must have a concrete and precise vision that tells you the direction in which you want to move and what you want to achieve. For example, if you are starting a new business, it is important that you decide how much you want to sell in the first year, how many customers you want to acquire, and what your financial goals will be.

Next, it is important to create a concrete plan. This plan provides a roadmap to achieve your goals. It should detail your marketing strategies, financial management, customer service, and other important aspects. While creating a plan, also keep in mind that your strategies are practical and implementable. You must ensure that you have the necessary resources, skills, and team support so that you can accomplish your goals.

You will face many challenges in your entrepreneurial journey —market competition, economic fluctuations, customer expectations, and more. To overcome these challenges, you will need patience, commitment, and persistent hard work. With well-set goals and a strong plan, you can overcome these challenges and move towards success.

Entrepreneurs like Aditya have proved that when you pursue your goals with honesty and hard work, you can definitely touch the heights of success. The basis of his success was the identification of clear goals, a solid plan, and perseverance and commitment throughout his journey. The same principles apply to your entrepreneurial journey as well.

When you set your entrepreneurial goals in a clear and measurable manner and make a solid plan to achieve those goals, success can come to you easily. Your hard work, dedication, and steps in the right direction can take your business to new heights. Successful entrepreneurs are those who stay dedicated to their goals and work continuously to achieve them despite difficulties.

# IS SUCCESS THE SAME AS WEALTH?

Success and wealth are two words that are often used together in our society. Many people believe that the one who has more money is the one who is truly successful. But, does success mean only wealth? Is it possible for a person to be rich but still not be successful, or a person to have less money but still be successful? To know the answer to these questions, we need to understand the difference between success and wealth in depth.

Money and success are often linked to each other, but they are not the same thing. Money is a means by which you can get material comforts in your life, but the meaning of success is much broader and deeper than that. The real meaning of success is in achieving your life goals, whether it is personal development, social service, contribution to art or science, or spending time with your family and friends. Money can be only a part, but it cannot be the only criterion of success.

Steve Jobs' name needs no introduction in the tech world. As co-founder of Apple, he not only built a successful company but also changed the way the world thought and worked. Jobs was extremely wealthy, but for him true success was not just about making money.

Steve Jobs emphasized many times during his life that his main goal was not to make money. For him, the true measure of success was his creativity and innovation. He said, "The amount of money I make is not the measure of my success. The true measure of my success is what I create and the legacy I leave behind." Jobs believed that his true success was in changing the world through Apple products, such as the iPhone, iPad, and MacBook.

The biggest lesson of Steve Jobs' life was that success does not mean only financial wealth, but doing something for the society that changes people's lives. When he was suffering from cancer and was in his last days of life, he said that the money he earned did not matter to him anymore. He realized that true success means contributing to society and creating a lasting legacy.

This aspect of Jobs' life shows that even if you have a lot of money, true success is when you positively impact society with your actions and thoughts.

Success is not just about money. People like Steve Jobs, John Wooden, Mother Teresa, and John D. Rockefeller have proven that true success is about self-satisfaction, contribution to society, and making a positive difference in the lives of others.

Money may be important, but it cannot be the only measure of success. True success comes when you achieve your life goals, find happiness and satisfaction in your work, and make a positive contribution to your society. If you are looking for true success, don't just run after money. Adopt values and principles in your life that bring happiness and satisfaction to you and others, and that is true success.

# NETWORKING RULES FOR NETWORKING

Success is a complex concept with many elements contributing to it. One of the most important elements is networking. Networking done right not only opens doors to new opportunities in your career and business, but also helps you reach heights where you can achieve your goals. But networking is not just about meeting people; it is a deep and effective process that requires trust, support, and building true relationships.

The friendship and professional relationship between Bill Gates and Warren Buffett is a classic example of success and networking. When Bill Gates and Warren Buffett first met in 1991, both realized that they had a deep connection and synergy of ideas. Although they were from two different fields—Bill Gates was a pioneer in the technology sector, while Warren Buffett was an expert in the field of finance and investments—they had similar values and approaches.

Buffett taught Gates the importance of long-term investing and financial discipline. Buffett had a vision of how success can be achieved through patience and smart investment decisions. Gates, on the other hand, helped Buffett understand the possibilities and risks in the world of technology. Gates showed Buffett how technology can not only transform businesses but also affect the entire world.

This relationship not only contributed to the personal growth of both individuals, but also greatly benefited their organizations. Warren Buffett decided to invest in Microsoft, and Bill Gates sought advice from Buffett in his philanthropic endeavors. Their partnership helped Gates and Buffett become even more successful in their respective fields. This example shows that through the right networking, you can build relationships with people who can make your life even more rich and successful.

Oprah Winfrey's name needs no introduction in the world. Coming from a poor family, she achieved a position that people around the world admire. But a large part of her success was possible only through networking. Oprah understood early in her career that connecting with the right people was extremely important for her. Through her talk show, The Oprah Winfrey Show, she not only got a chance to connect with big celebrities and influential people, but also built deep and strong relationships with them.

Oprah understood that her show was not just a means of entertainment but also a platform through which she could bring about positive change in society. She invited experts from various fields, social activists, and the world's most influential people on her show and made their views reach millions of people. This not only led to an increase in the popularity of her show but also strengthened Oprah's personal and professional network.

The influence of this network can be seen in various aspects of her life. When Oprah expanded her networking and connecting with people, she started working on important issues like education, health, and social justice. Her effective network helped her become a global icon and strengthened her presence in every corner of society.

• When you connect with someone, be genuine and honest. People will like you only when they feel that you are honest and genuine.

• Networking is not only about knowing others, but also about learning from them. Everyone has something new to teach.

• Help and support the people in your network. This strengthens relationships and builds trust.

• Networking is a long-term process. You have to develop it slowly and over time.

• Networking should not be just a one-way process. Both parties should benefit from it. The people connecting with you also want to learn something from you, and also want to get your help.

• Right networking means connecting with the right people. It is not necessary that you should try to connect with everyone. You should connect with people who are important to your goals and who can contribute to your journey.

Networking is a major secret of success, but to adopt it correctly, you have to build true and honest relationships. People like Bill Gates, Warren Buffett, Oprah Winfrey, Richard Branson, and Elon Musk have achieved extraordinary success in their lives by using networking correctly.

When you also adopt these rules of networking and connect with people with a true heart, it can become the key to success for you. Remember, networking is not just a medium to meet new people, but it is a platform that can help you discover new opportunities, adopt new ideas, and take your business and life to new heights.

# SUCCESS MEANS ENJOYING

Once upon a time, there lived a man named John in a small town in America. John was a simple farmer, but there was one great thing about his life—he was always happy and content. He did not have much money, nor any great possessions, but he always smiled and enjoyed his work.

John's childhood friend, Robert, who had worked very hard in his studies, had become a big businessman. He lived in the big city, lived in a luxurious house, and his company was famous all over the world. Robert had made a lot of money, but there was one thing missing in his life—he was never completely satisfied. He always tried to get more, but the more he earned, the more he wanted more.

One day, Robert thought he would visit his old friend John. He thought how many problems John must be facing in his short life and limited means. He thought that John would probably ask him for help, and he would help him by giving him some money.

Robert drove to John's village in his luxurious car. When he reached there, he saw John sitting under a tree laughing, with children playing around him, and his wife tending to the flowers in their garden. John welcomed Robert warmly and invited him inside his house.

The two friends talked for a long time. Robert saw that John was really very happy, and he did not lack anything in his life. Robert asked him, "John, how can you be so happy? You do not have much money, nor any big property."

John smiled and replied, "Robert, you are right, I don't have much money, but I am completely satisfied with what I have. I work on my farm, spend time with my family, and enjoy every moment of my life. For me, success does not mean only wealth, but enjoying life and being satisfied."

Robert heard this and got thinking. He realized that he had achieved a lot in his life, but he never enjoyed his life. He always tried to get more, but he was never able to be happy. He thought that maybe John was right—true success means enjoying life and being content, no matter how much wealth you have or not.

After that day, Robert made some changes in his life. He cut back a little on his work, started spending more time with his family, and started finding happiness in the little things. Gradually, he also started enjoying life like John and he realized that this is what true success means.

The lesson from this story is that ultimately, the real meaning of success is to enjoy life and be content. No matter how much wealth you have, if you are not able to enjoy your life, then that success is incomplete. The satisfaction that comes from the little joys of life is true success.

# AN INSPIRING EXAMPLE FROM ITALY

Montepulciano, a beautiful village in the Tuscany region of Italy, is famous for its rich wines and lush grapes. In this village lived a simple farmer named Antonio. Antonio's life was very simple, but there was one special thing about him—he was completely satisfied and happy with his life. His winery was small, but he had a deep love for his work.

Antonio was born in this village and from childhood he started helping his father in growing grapes. His father taught him that only hard work and honest work brings real happiness in life. Antonio made these things the main mantra of his life. He would tend the grapes all day, make wine, and spend time in the evening having dinner with his family. His life was simple, but there was no lack of happiness and satisfaction in it.

On the other hand, Luca, who lived in Rome, was a very big businessman. Luca had worked very hard in his life and gradually became the owner of one of the largest winery companies in Italy. He had no shortage of money, but still he was never completely happy. He was always striving for more. He had a large team at his winery that ran his business, but Luca was always looking for new opportunities.

Luca had heard that there were some old and famous wineries in the villages of Montepulciano that still made wine using traditional methods. He thought that if he bought these wineries, his business could grow even bigger. To this end, Luca decided to travel to Montepulciano.

When Luca arrived in the village, he saw how peaceful and beautiful the place was. The people here were simple and happy. He visited many wineries, and finally, he arrived at Antonio's winery. He saw Antonio sitting in the courtyard of his winery inspecting the quality of the grapes. Antonio welcomed Luca warmly and agreed to show him the winery.

Luca visited the winery and saw how passionately and hardworking Antonio was at his work. He saw that every grape of Antonio matured under his supervision and his wine had a unique sweetness. Luca immediately decided that he wanted to buy this winery.

He went to Antonio and said to him, "Antonio, your winery is so wonderful. I want to buy it. I will give you a huge amount of money in exchange for it, which will change your life. Why are you wasting your time in this small village, when you can go to the city and live a comfortable life?"

Antonio smiled and replied, "Thank you, Luca, but I don't want to sell this winery. I am completely happy with my life. For me success does not mean only money. I get happiness from my work, and that is the biggest success for me. I enjoy my work here and that is the source of my satisfaction."

Luca did not believe Antonio's words. He thought that perhaps Antonio did not understand what a big opportunity he was missing. He said to Antonio, "But Antonio, what have you gained by staying in this village? You can go to the city and earn more money, create a big property. Don't you think that this will make your life even better?"

Antonio responded seriously, "Luca, what I have achieved in my life cannot be measured by wealth alone. For me, working with my grapes every day, making wine, and spending time with my family—that is true happiness. I get satisfaction from what I do, and that is my success. If I ran after money like you, I might lose this happiness and satisfaction."

Luca heard this and went into deep thought. He reflected on his life and found that he always tried to achieve more, but was never fully satisfied. He realized that he never enjoyed his success and always lived in stress and dissatisfaction.

Luca decided to make a change in his life that day. He handed over the responsibility of parts of his company to his colleagues and took time for himself to spend time with his family and enjoy life. He realized that true success does not mean only wealth and possessions, but the contentment and happiness that one feels in every moment of life.

This true story of Antonio and Luca teaches us that ultimately, success means enjoying and being content. No matter how much money you have, if you are not able to enjoy your life, then that success is incomplete. We should learn to understand and enjoy the little joys of life, because that is the real success.

www.ingramcontent.com/pod-product-compliance
Lightning Source LLC
Chambersburg PA
CBHW020442220526
45464CB00002B/819